MW00476985

A NEW BOOK RELEASE

A LOVE FOREVER
Creating An Amazing Marriage

by
Lynne Thomas, M.A.

Just For You! ... A free gift

Please tell your friends about the book!

To order copies, contact:

Lakeshore.press@ymail.com
or
Amazon.com

The ultimate gift is to give love.
The ultimate reward is to receive love.
~ Joyce Brothers

A LOVE FOREVER

Creating An *Amazing* Marriage

LYNNE THOMAS

LP
Michigan   Arizona

A LOVE FOREVER   Copyright © 2015 by Lynne Thomas
Publication Date: February 30, 2016

All rights reserved. Printed in the United States of America, no part of this book can be reproduced or transmitted in any form or by any means, mechanical or electronic, including recording and photocopying, or by any information storage and retrieval methods, without permission in writing from author or publisher except in the case of brief quotations embodied in critical articles and reviews. The author and the publisher are not making any representation or warranties about the exactness or completeness of the information in this work, and specifically disclaim entirely all warranties, which include without limitation warranties of appropriateness for particular purpose. No warranty can be created or offered by sales and/or promotional materials. Ideas, advice, and strategies included herein may not be suitable for every person, or couple, or marriage, or family. This work is sold with the knowledge and understanding that the author and publisher are not involved in providing legal services, psychological or psychiatric treatment or services, marriage counseling or professional services. If psychological treatment, psychiatric treatment, professional help, or marriage counseling are required or needed, the services of a competent mental health professional should be sought.

Scripture quotations marked NIV are from the New International Version of the Bible.

To schedule Lynne Thomas for a speaking engagement, visit
www.marriageamazing.com

For additional information about this book, contact Lakeshore Press
LakeshorePress@ymail.com

Library of Congress Control Number: 2015905292

ISBN – 13:   978-0-692-41938-0
ISBN – 10:   0-692-41938-1

Dedicated to my sons who have always encouraged
me and filled my heart with love
and wonderful memories.

~~~

Dedicated to all the lovely couples, friends,
and families who inspired me to write this book.

ACKNOWLEDGEMENTS

Thank you to all the wonderful people
who made this book possible.

CONTENTS

CONTENTS

Love is patient; love is kind.
It does not envy, it does not boast,
it is not proud. It does not dishonor others,
it is not self-seeking, it is not easily angered;
it keeps no record of wrongs. Love does not
delight in evil but rejoices with
the truth. It always protects,
always trusts, always hopes,
always perseveres.

1 Corinthians 13:4-7 (NIV)

A LOVE FOREVER

PREFACE

An incredible joy exists when a couple improves or transforms their marriage. The inspiration for this book comes from many joy filled couples, eager for family and friends to equally experience a rewarding marriage. At the same time, there was a wonderful excitement in my own heart to share with every married couple a book filled with practical effective loving wisdom that can transform a marriage.

As a marriage counselor and therapist who enjoyed working with married couples for over thirty years, I also delighted in leading seminars, speaking to audiences, and instructing groups. During these knowledge-based events, it was clear to me that the participants valued the wisdom and insight that specific ideas offer, notably when accompanied by action steps. Participants welcomed this format. For this reason, I was eager to use the same engaging format in this book.

As you can see, this book is not marriage counseling, psychotherapy or any type of psychological or psychiatric treatment. If you and your spouse need these services, please contact a marriage counselor or a mental health professional such as a psychologist or psychiatrist.

However, if you are a married couple who wants to enrich or enhance your marriage, this book will provide you with some effective ideas. Your vital first step is to make a decision to take full responsibility for the change your marriage may need. It is your effort that will bring about the change, you desire. In other words, your success will stem from your own choices and actions.

Each day you and your spouse are creating your lives, creating your relationship, and creating your marriage with the choices you make. The key is making positive effective choices that elevate every aspect of your relationship, marriage, and life.

My hope is that this book will serve as a dynamic resource of ideas and inspiration as you select new choices to make your love enduring and your marriage amazing.

Wishing you the very best,
Lynne

INTRODUCTION

If one moves confidently in the direction of one's dreams,
and strives to live the life imagined, one will
meet with an unexpected success.
~ Henry David Thoreau

This book is about choices, the real change agents in a person's life and in a marriage. This book takes loving choices and makes them visible, active, creative, gratifying, and motivating. In a mysterious way, loving, sincere choices become the Potter's wheel; altering uniquely the marriage by enriching it, enhancing it, and transforming it.

Within the pages of this book are meaningful concepts and practical ideas, designed to inspire couples to look through a new lens to select true loving choices. As the quality of a couple's choices elevate, so does the quality of a couple's experiences. The more loving, enriching, and creative their choices become, the more deeply gratifying their togetherness becomes. As the marriage evolves into a place that brings out the best in the couple, the bonds that connect them strengthen. The marriage becomes fulfilling, loving, and more valuable to the couple. This rewarding experience and new awareness inspire new effort and a greater commitment to the marriage as the couple moves forward.

For this reason, a couple's most important asset is a clear understanding of the way loving choices create successful changes in every aspect of a marriage. Every loving choice produces a positive result, a positive effect, and a positive outcome.

On the contrary, a negative choice produces a negative result, a negative effect, and a negative outcome. Too many negative outcomes tend to have a destructive impact on a couple's marriage, their love, and their future. Immersed and surrounded by negativity, a healthy marriage and a healthy love are unable to thrive.

It's wise for a couple to learn how to solve problems and differences, with a positive strategy that produces a reassuring result and grows their love.

HOW THIS BOOK IS ORGANIZED

As you read through this book, notice how it is divided into four sections. Each section prepares you for the following section. One idea builds on the next. All four sections work together to provide ideas for loving choices as you grow and enrich your marriage.

The first section introduces an inspiring perspective, a point of view that opens the door for change and encourages a willingness to try. Each choice in this section presents a refreshing outlook for you to consider and embrace, as you prepare to actively enhance your marriage. These ideas invite you to think differently and to stretch beyond anger or indifference. As a first step in preparation for an experience of love in action, a couple must leave negatives behind, and welcome a more pleasant emotion into their relationship.

Turning to the second section, the focus is on a couple's past. More specifically, it addresses the couple's marital history, while offering positive choices and steps for a spouse to implement; making loving adjustments in the present. This section helps each spouse to modify to some degree unpleasant memories from the past. This shift in perspective can prevent negative memories from impacting a spouse's immediate experience as well as future expectations. In addition, the significant choices in this second section, when implemented provide love with an opportunity to grow and deepen in noteworthy ways.

The third section emphasizes the present. This segment offers loving choices that elevate a couple's daily interaction adding unexpected value to the marriage. Daily interaction that may include conflict, decision–making, communication, differences, and other important aspects of a couple's marital interaction. New favorable choices provide a refreshing opportunity, while strengthening a couple's love and shifting the couple's focus. As the couple actively embraces their unique creativity, successful solutions, valuable experiences, and wonderful memories, they can acknowledge incredible change taking place.

Creativity is the secret to creating an amazing marriage. Taking every day events and making them special, with an attention to detail and a sense of the big picture; makes the present moment a treasured experience.

Now, a couple's energy and efforts are invested in creating outstanding positive experiences and fulfilling outcomes, at the same time removing boredom, minimizing anger, negative interaction, and building a more enduring marriage.

The Appendix of the book provides some special resources. The first resource provides beneficial worksheets to measure your personal progress with specific choices. The second resource offers you noteworthy worksheets for identifying and solving problems. Although, it is the most significant task to complete, the best results spring forth when consideration is exercised. This will help you minimize the length of time spent with problems, and shift your attention to solutions.

The third resource presents magnificent events, terrific joy filled experiences, and extraordinary places to select from as you and your spouse make creative plans for wonderful trips or vacations or date-nights.

HOW TO GET STARTED

One of the easiest ways to begin is for each spouse to simply read this book quietly alone. Unlike many books, this book is about taking positive personal action, and not about spending your time discussing the ideas in the book. This unique approach, allows each spouse to implement new choices independently while producing positive outcomes in the marriage.

In other words, each spouse's individual choices and actions will give birth to meaningful changes in their marital relationship.

More specifically, if each spouse begins the book at the same time independently, works on the same choice individually for a week, then continues in this manner each week; the outcome becomes very rewarding for a couple.

As each spouse develops new loving choices, these new loving choices elevate the marriage to a new level. Undeniably, as a couple, this is quite fascinating and rewarding to observe.

Continuing in this manner as you work your way through the book, allows loving choices to transform your marriage. By implementing love filled choices, undesirable behaviors and harmful words shrink from the marriage as love becomes more powerful and predominate.

Reaching the end of the book, your most important indicator of success is certainly the rewarding changes you and your spouse have produced, without conflict, debate, or offense. As a couple, your sincere effort, self-motivation, eagerness to learn new ideas, and ability to implement new choices; collectively have the power to make your marital relationship incredibly rewarding.

A WORD TO THE WISE

Yes, the ideas in this book are very effective. Couples who are receptive to new ideas, able to execute choices, prepared to be patient as change unfolds, and ready to persist with their efforts, have an opportunity to enhance, enrich, or change their marriages. That is my heartfelt hope and desire for you and your spouse.

On the flip side, there are some specific marriages, in which this self-help approach may not be appropriate; other options may be necessary, and much more suitable and effective for these marriages. These couples might benefit from the services of a mental health professional such as a marriage counselor, or perhaps a psychotherapist or psychiatrist. These are important considerations, because this book is not marriage counseling or therapy or any type of mental health treatment.

However, for those motivated couples who are ready to take personal action and who are prepared to implement new choices; this book is a great choice. Stay motivated, work independently, maintain a positive attitude, allow love to guide you, and remain persistent, as you embrace new choices. This is your life, valuable and priceless. Create an amazing marriage, by making loving choices that elevate your interaction, deepen your love, cultivate your experiences, and breathes new life into your relationship.

Start Now!

The happiness in your life is determined by the quality of your thoughts.

~Marcus Aurelius

PART ONE

A New Perspective

*We cannot solve our problems with the same
level of thinking that created them.*
~ Albert Einstein

Choice

1

MAKING CHOICES

*Our lives are the sum total of the
choices we have made.*

~ Wayne Dyer

Creating an amazing marriage is an invitation for you
and your spouse to gently grip your marriage with both
hands, and turn it around. Shaping it into a marriage you
can live in, love in, grow in, and enjoy, all the time
forming a lasting love.

But wait! Are you thinking something quite different?
Perhaps, you're thinking, "Marriages don't change. People
don't change." If these are your thoughts, you're not alone, so
pervasive are these beliefs that married couples make
decisions based on them. This is very unfortunate!

The power of a belief is fascinating. Think of it, if you
believe that marriages don't change, you're left with no
options to improve your marriage. Blinded by this belief,
and clearly cut off from new possibilities, you might find
yourself resisting positive change, distancing yourself
from your spouse, feeling hopeless, struggling to stay in
the marriage, or continuing unproductive behavior. All the
time, thinking your marriage is the problem, when the real
culprit may be your belief system; a belief system that does
not allow for new ideas or a positive perspective.

Consider this incredible fact: At birth, every person is given time, space, and choices. With these three tools, each person designs their life, shapes experiences, forms relationships, cultivates their career, makes personal changes, and develops their marriage.

Choices are remarkable invisible agents of change in every person's life. An extremely valuable creative tool, choices have the power to bring forth new experiences, successful progress, and incredible outcomes.

Your first step to enriching, enhancing, or transforming your marriage is to explore the idea that your marriage can change with your new extraordinary choices.

As each spouse in a marriage selects and implements new positive choices, change results, new experiences occur; the marriage takes on new positive qualities. With time and consistent, active, positive effort, a couple can alter their marriage. Spouses can fill their marriage with joy, new experiences, great interactions, and incredible love.

By changing your beliefs, and embracing the idea that your choices are the real change agents in your life, you and your spouse can create an amazing marriage and a love forever.

~ Make a choice to create an amazing marriage ~

Choice

2

MENTAL-FLASHLIGHT

The greatest discovery of my generation is that
individuals can alter their lives, by
changing their attitude.

~ William James

Your attention is powerful, indispensible, and vital; it determines the content of your experiences, the quality of your life, and ultimately your attitude about your marriage.

In many ways, your personal attention is like a mental flashlight that you shine on things, people, and situations. Your experience of reality, at any given moment is contingent upon where you direct your attention, where you shine your mental-flashlight. Whatever you shine your mental-flashlight on, fills your mind, and becomes your experience at the moment.

In a marriage, there is a tendency to shine and keep your mental-flashlight on the negatives in your marital relationship or on your spouse's flaws. These negatives become your point of reference. The lens through, which you view your spouse and marriage. A mental focus that produces negative emotions and damaging attitudes.

Can you see how significant your attention is to the success of your marriage? Ask yourself, "What am I shining my mental flashlight on?"

Your challenge as a spouse is to direct your attention; in other words, focus your mental flashlight on things of substance and value. Of course, you can stay aware of negatives, but don't give negatives your consistent persistent attention. Remind yourself that in a marriage nothing of value flows from negative thinking, negative actions, or a negative attitude.

Consider this idea: One person goes through life shining their mental-flashlight on flaws and mistakes, another person goes through life shining their mental flashlight on their resentment and pain, still another person goes through life shining their mental flashlight on their plans and goals. In the end, each person will have had a different experience of life, a different quality of life, and a different outcome.

Your attention is magnificent, incredible, and unique. Focus on things of value and substance in order to improve your attitude, enhance your marriage, elevate the quality of your life, and achieve the best possible outcome.

~ Make a choice to focus on things of value ~

Choice

3

A POSITIVE PERCEPTION

*Today, you are where your thoughts have
taken you, tomorrow you will be
where your thoughts place you.*

~James Allen

Each spouse in a marriage has a very personal experience of events in the marriage. Of course, they do! This is why. As individuals, we focus on a specific situation or a particular conversation. Then, privately we talk to ourselves about the specific event. In a very unique way, the event, as well as our self-talk about the event merge in our memory, becoming our experience of the event.

Even though, the couple focuses on the same event or conversation, his or her self-talk is different, which produces a different memory of the event.

Without realizing it, we react emotionally to our internal conversation, our self-talk. Yet, we mistakenly believe that we are reacting emotionally to the event itself.

Do you notice how your self-talk adds another dimension to your experience of an event? Actually, your internal conversation modifies the event in a significant way by adding additional information to the event.

Clearly, your self-talk is a crucial part of how you view an experience, as it gives additional meaning to the event.

Consider this idea. If your self-talk about an event is negative, your understanding of the event is negative. If your internal conversation about an event is positive, your memory of the event is positive.

It's important to understand that your self-talk together with the emotions it produces, becomes your experience of the event. This process is a blind spot for most spouses.

In a marriage, if a couple hopes to find happiness or experience more pleasure in life, it will be necessary for each spouse to keep their thoughts pleasant, hopeful, encouraging, and on the positive side. A major part of your reality takes place in our mind. The quality and content of your experience is directly related to the quality and content of your thoughts, and the quality of your emotional reaction to your thoughts.

Take some time and listen to your internal conversation. Remember, self-talk that has a positive focus helps you to make positive choices. Make an effort to select an internal conversation that enhances your life, pulls you forward, provides solutions, and allows you to experience life in new and better ways.

Positive thoughts dramatically alter the direction of your life. They offer new outcomes, new experiences, and new insights that can grow your love and enrich your future.

~ Make a choice to select positive thoughts ~

Choice

4

THE COMMITMENT

Experience is not what happens to a man;
but it's what a man does with
what happens to him.

~Aldous Huxley

One of the most valuable questions you can ask yourself at this moment, "Am I willing to commit 100 percent to transforming or enriching my marriage?" Certainly, a significant question requires a definite answer.

By making a commitment to improve your marriage, you are investing in your life and your future. Being "all in" with your commitment means you're agreeing to give 100 percent of dedication, effort, motivation, thought, persistence, and receptivity to improving and transforming your marriage. In the process, your commitment will benefit your marriage, your future, your life, your spouse, and you personally. Your commitment will create incredible value.

Have you ever noticed how life is designed so that it gives each person another chance to make a better choice, another chance to have a better result, another chance to correct a mistake, and another chance to turn things around? Life gives everyone unlimited chances to create amazing choices. Why not utilize this incredible opportunity? As people, we are always creating, always choosing, and always initiating change. It's true!

Our choices not only create change, but they move us forward or backward; choices produce for us positive or negative outcomes, and in a very mysterious way, they create experiences that mold and shape us as individuals.

You are not only creating your daily experiences with your choices, but you are creating your marriage, you are creating your life, and you are creating your personal characteristics. This is a fascinating truth to consider.

Your full commitment to enhance your marriage is one of the best and most valuable decisions you can make for yourself and for your marriage.

~ Make a choice to give 100% of effort to your marriage ~

Choice

5

LOVE IN ACTION

To love and to be loved is like feeling
the sun from both sides.
~David Viscott

In the famous musical *My Fair Lady,* Eliza Doolittle exclaimed, "If you love me, don't just talk about it, show me with your actions."

Of course, we know exactly what she means. Think of it, when love is an action it fills a marriage, the marriage takes on a new dimension, and new characteristics. Because love is a radiant, wonderful, caring, life-giving energy that brings out the best in whatever it fills, people and events are elevated to new incredible levels.

Love is difficult to define, amazing to experience and easy to embrace. The challenge every married couple faces is this one, to keep their love alive by nurturing it, growing it, and protecting it. At the same time, preventing resentment, anger, deception, apathy, distrust, and disrespect from slowly slipping into the marital relationship. These negatives are destructive to a marriage.

But, by embracing love, letting it spill over onto everything, a couple invites amazing experiences into their marriage. It is magnificent when love fills a person, and that person allows love to flow through their conversations, affecting their words, their ideas, and their responses. Love becomes the intangible substance of their marriage.

Love's unique nature can move through our actions and reactions, bringing us closer together in deep significant joyful ways. Love's mysterious nature can move through our thoughts and reasoning, allowing us to work in harmony and creatively solving our problems. Love's expansive nature can flow through a married couple's cooperative efforts, producing rewarding results and incredible creativity.

The influence and effects of love are tremendous, especially for married couples. Priceless and irreplaceable, love is a key to marital success when it's put into action.

~ Make a choice to demonstrate your love ~

PART TWO

DEALING WITH THE PAST

Change is a principle of life. Individuals who look only to the past are sure to miss the future.

~ John F. Kennedy

Choice

6

PROBLEMS

*Each problem is a valuable gift; without
them, we wouldn't grow.*

~ Anthony Robbins

Certainly, you would agree, problems are a real mystery and frequently a challenge. They pop-up at the most unexpected times; catching us off guard, leaving us worried and concerned. It may be hard to perceive these unforeseen intruders as gifts or positive influences in a marriage or a life. But, they truly are!

Surprisingly, problems signal that a change is needed. Problems indicate we're moving in the wrong direction, and that if we don't take action things may become worse.

More specifically, when a problem surfaces in some area of your marriage, it means a change is needed in that area. The sooner you and your spouse make a change, the sooner the problem disappears. Problems stick around and reoccur when no action is taken to resolve them or change things.

Think for a moment about this fact: Problems are uniquely woven into the very fiber of our lives. Every person receives problems. At this very moment, every person is either at the beginning, at the middle, at the end of a problem, or in a waiting period, until the next problem shows up.

Since problems are an ongoing part of life and an on

going part of a marriage; it's extremely important for you and your spouse to make a choice to become problem solvers. In other words, a problem solving team, focused on sharing ideas and possible solutions, until an appropriate solution is uncovered and put into practice. Unresolved problems pile up, creating oppressive outcomes, leaving no room for happiness, love, fun, or progress.

As a couple, never lose sight of the fact that problems need solutions, and the quicker you solve your problems the more time you and your spouse have to enjoy each other, share new experiences, and achieve wonderful goals.

The secret to problems is to find solutions and learn from your problems. Notice problems motivate you to quickly ask questions, research information, seek out experts for advice, think differently, and make new choices.

As a married couple, become exceptional problem solvers, working together to find terrific solutions for your problems.

~ Make a choice to become a problem solving team ~

Choice

7

REMOVING ANGER

A heart full of anger has no space for love.

~ Joan Lunden

In a marriage, sooner or later one spouse or both spouses feel angry. The reason might be crushed expectations, emotional pain, or some type of negative experience. In any case, when anger is present, it has a negative effect on each spouse and the marriage. A swift change is needed. When we're angry, it seems natural to hang on to the very memories that are hurting us. In time, our pain starts weighting us down. We find ourselves stuck, clinging to anger, resentment, blame, or remorse, continually reviewing the injustices, and suffering all the while. Held captive by our own thoughts and pain, cut off from joy, love, and motivation. What a predicament for a marriage!

Even more destructive to the future of a marriage is a spouse's decision to allow anger to determine his or her words, actions, reactions, or decisions.

The best way spouses might put the brakes on anger is to shift their attention from their hurt feelings to a positive resolution. In other words, spending their energy thinking of a fair and acceptable resolution to the experience is the best choice. Keeping in mind that the event that caused the upset no longer exists, only a memory remains of the event.

To impact your memory in a positive way, find an optimistic reaction, and implement it. Create a positive change, make a positive choice.

By asking one specific question, a couple may find the best resolution. Consider this question: What do you want for your pain or disappointment? The answer may be a specific agreement, a certain correction, an apology, an explanation, or even a gift. It's up to the couple to find the best solution and implement it as soon as possible. Remind yourself that love is the goal of your marriage, and getting even or hurting each other time after time will not create an enduring love. It will be wise to move quickly to return your relationship and marital interaction to a state of love and harmony.

As a couple, if anger has harmed your relationship in the past, make a choice now to put the brakes on anger. Agree to resolve your altercations as soon as they occur, so you can truly embrace love now, and enjoy a meaningful future. In other words, select love over anger and create a rewarding outcome.

~ Make a choice to stop getting angry ~

Choice

8

LET IT GO

Forgiveness means letting the past go.
~ Gerald Jampolsky

In a marriage, forgiveness clears the way for love to bloom, so nothing obstructs love's movement. Sure enough, love is alive, growing, changing, and developing, especially when it unites with forgiveness in a marriage. Unique and necessary, love and forgiveness provide the foundation for a long-term relationship.

The challenge for many couples is to make forgiveness away of life, a welcomed process, a positive choice, and a valuable component to their marriage. Couples must understand that life provides many wonderful things, and life also provides imperfection. Yes, imperfection. That aspect of life that is rarely discussed, barely accepted, and hardly understood.

One of the distinct qualities of forgiveness is that you must put it into practice to understand its true value. However, if you haven't practiced forgiveness, the first time you attempt to forgive your spouse, the experience may grip you like eating the seeds of a jalapeno pepper. Everything in you wants to resist going through with it. The fact that your spouse hurt you, and goes unpunished, may make forgiveness an unappealing process. This is the sticking point. Couples get stuck right here.

This is the key, forgiveness allows your spouse to give you another chance, and it allows you to give your spouse another chance. It's a fair process, a positive choice, and a successful method of letting go. Releasing the event from your memory, so love and happiness are possible again.

The past doesn't exist, the hurtful experience doesn't exist; you can't change it or alter it. The hurtful experience is only a memory. All you can really do that's healthy is release the hurtful memory. That's right, let it go, clear your mind of the memory. Certainly, you can discuss the matter as a couple, make choices to change and improve future experiences.

As a couple, if your un-forgiveness created problems for your marriage in the past, embrace forgiveness now, make a choice to bring forgiveness into your marital relationship and change your future.

Forgiveness is a gift a couple gives to their marriage. A gift given sincerely, which frees each spouse to pour love and happiness into their relationship in wonderful ways. Love and forgiveness work together to create an enduring love, a love forever.

~ Make a choice to forgive your spouse ~

Choice

9

APOLOGIZING

Never let an excuse ruin an apology.

~ Benjamin Franklin

In a marriage, a heartfelt apology can heal a painful experience and revitalize a spouse's spirit. A sincere apology says you regret your actions and you regret the pain you caused. Think of it, owning your mistakes openly and honestly is an act of integrity, a gesture of love that can alter a spouse's memory of the past in a positive way.

On the flip side, if you're feeling some resistance now, stop and ask yourself, "What belief is encouraging your resistance?" Perhaps, it's the idea that apologizing is a sign of weakness. This unrealistic belief may cause major problems in your relationship.

Refusing to apologize, a prideful excuse or a stubborn denial sends a message that your hurtful actions were intentional. Receiving this type of message from your spouse is a real arrow to the heart. Strong with an offense, feeble with the truth, certainly undermines your marital relationship.

A long-term marriage needs forgiveness and apologies to maintain its health and love. The best way to apologize is to find a quiet moment and talk privately or write a sincere letter of apology. If there are things you need to apologize for make a choice to offer an apology now. If you have a tendency to make an excuse for your hurtful behavior, or quickly minimize your unkind actions, or perhaps swiftly make it someone else's fault; stop yourself and tell the truth. Remember, your relationship needs to include honest and trust to grow and thrive.

It might be beneficial to present your offenses to your spouse in person, apologizing for each one individually; if you haven't done so before now. Keep in mind, by apologizing you are healing your spouse's memory of the past, healing your history with your spouse, and healing your marriage.

Make a choice now to continue your apologies to enhance the future of your marriage. A heartfelt apology has the potential to breathe new life into a marital relationship.

~ Make a choice to apologize to your spouse ~

Choice

10

MAKING ASSUMPTIONS

Do not assume. Ask questions.
~ Bonnie Smith

One remarkable way of thinking is making assumptions. Simply, it's the process of accepting our own thoughts about an event as the truth, without proof. Even more intriguing is the fact that we react emotionally to our assumptions, make decisions based on our assumptions, and proceed with specific actions based on our assumptions.

Assumptions play a huge part in the arguments and misunderstandings in a marriage. Most spouses are unaware of the assumptions they make, and the impact these assumptions have on their marital relationship.

Here is a brief example of how assumptions create problems in a marriage. In your imagination, envision that your spouse is late for dinner. (*This is the event.*) You tell yourself that he is being deliberately inconsiderate. (*This is your assumption.*) Every time you notice the time, you are filled with thoughts of his inconsideration. (*This is how you attach your assumptions to the event.*) Your assumptions make you extremely angry. (*This is your emotional reaction to your assumptions.*) In one of your angry moments, you send him a heated text message. (*This is your action based on your emotional reaction to your assumptions.*)

You notice that he didn't respond to your text message. You think to yourself that he is ignoring your message. (This is another assumption.)

Soon, he arrives home, unlocks the door, and you blast him with your anger. Finally, when things calm down, he explains that he became ill while driving, pulled off the road, and tried to rest to regain some stability before driving again. During this time, his cell phone needed to be charged, but he was too sick to charge it. (*This is the truth.*)

As you can see, by acting on your assumptions, treating them as the truth, you created a problem that made your spouse feel hurt, falsely accused, and misunderstood.

To eliminate problems in your marriage caused by assumptions, make a choice to clarify and confirm your assumptions in the future.

One approach is to ask questions to gain knowledge of the facts. Another useful method is to present your assumptions to your spouse and see if they're correct. These methods have huge benefits for your marital relationship and your future.

~ Make a choice to stop making assumptions ~

Choice

11

CONFLICT

*Arguments, which are totally useless, embitter
human life more than anything else.*
~ Thomas Jefferson

Viewing the film, *Who's Afraid of Virginia Woolf* will give you a clear, vivid, dramatic picture of the destructive nature of marital conflict. Of course, this motion picture is extreme in every way. But, very helpful in exhibiting how consistently saying mean things and doing mean things will create a destructive environment that blocks out happiness and fulfillment. Certainly, insulting words, crude jabs, intimidating gestures, and offensive yelling sooner or later destroys love and rips the marriage apart.

Clearly, some marriages have conflict that is more indirect; while other marriages have emotional blow-ups whenever a spouse is not getting their way. If this is the case in your marriage, remove conflict by making a choice to omit certain offensive demeaning words from your vocabulary. Next, make a choice to eliminate rude yelling and other upsetting inappropriate behavior from your interaction with your spouse.

Instead of *acting out your anger*, tell your spouse how you feel with words; calmly express how you feel, simply say, "I'm angry." Then, in the same calm manner explain the reason for your anger without casting blame or guilt on your spouse. Remember, love is kind.

Of course, this pivotal event in your marriage will impact the future of your relationship for the better. Learning to express your thoughts and feelings in a calm reasonable way, with words that create an understanding for your spouse is true communication. Words that don't put your spouse on the defensive or on the attack, but encourages your spouse to be receptive to your message.

By proceeding in this manner, you open the door for a positive resolution, a more trusting relationship, a deeper intimacy, and an enduring love.

~ Make a choice to remove conflict from your marriage ~

Choice

12

CRITICISM

*I've traveled the world and I've never
observed a statue of a critic.*

~ Leonard Bernstein

Have you ever received a criticism that caught you by surprise? A gripping kind of experience that hurts and shocks at the same time stops you in your tracks. This type of criticism has no place in your marriage. It shuts down intimacy and pushes your spouse away. Eventually, destroying the love your spouse has for you, as it is more hurtful than helpful. Of course, this is not the only type of criticism.

Are you familiar with constant, consistent critical comments? Like a painful toothache, the whole thing becomes unbearable. No spouse wants to be greeted with his or her failures and flaws everyday. The impact of this type of criticism on a spouse's self-esteem, emotions, and spirit is enormously harmful. As a matter of fact, this constant, consistent, hurtful communication drives spouses away, far away; this is the underlying cause for numerous divorces. As a result, it is extremely important to make a choice to be considerate and supportive as a spouse.

Have you ever experienced criticism as "put-downs" or critical jokes? Criticism wrapped in anger is meant to hurt; this is dreadfully serious.

Make a shift from a negative method of expressing your opinions to a more positive expression. It's important to strive for kindness and consideration as you present your thoughts and suggestions to your spouse.

The best way to inspire a change or motivate your spouse to make a new choice is to use a positive approach. Select a positive way of presenting your words that does not pierce or sting.

One technique is to say what you *like,* instead of what you dislike. For example: As your wife is selecting something to wear, you might consider saying, "You look pretty in the peach dress." Instead of saying, "Please don't wear the blue pants." In this way, your spouse has the final say, while feeling good about either choice.

As a couple, if your marital relationship has suffered in the past because of your criticism, make a choice to change your future by removing criticism from your communication. Allow your words to express love, even as you are presenting helpful suggestions. Be sensitive to your spouse's feelings and sensitive to the effect your words have on your marriage and the future of your marital relationship.

~ Make a choice to stop criticizing your spouse ~

POWER STRUGGLES

It's not enough to discuss peace, you need to
believe in it and work at it.

~ Eleanor Roosevelt

What is a power struggle? Quite simply, that courageous attempt by one spouse or both, to successfully upset or hurt their spouse, in order to feel powerful, to be right, to be in control, or to win is a power struggle. These reoccurring interactions, propelled by anger and resentment, undermine the relationship. These damaging encounters threaten the survival of the marriage by destroying love and blocking compatibility. Power struggles destroy marriages.

Various behaviors comprise a power struggle, consider a few examples: Constantly fighting about the same problems, using the silent treatment, confronting your spouse using obscene words, deliberately insulting your spouse, fighting in front of others, holding a grudge and getting even, fighting while drinking, being manipulative, or intimidating your spouse. As you can see, nothing productive or beneficial comes from these behaviors.

If these toxic behaviors are a part of your interaction or conversation, extinguish them as soon as possible. They will only create a broken relationship that no one wants to be a part of or spend their life in.

Make a choice to change the future of your marriage by opening a door for love, and selecting behaviors that create harmony, trust, intimacy, and fulfillment.

At best, being friends is the most gratifying way to go through life as a married couple. Working to build trust, brings you closer together, makes your togetherness move into a more enduring future. It also provides an avenue for the marriage to change and grow over time, making communication a delight.

Sincere, kind, enjoyable interaction is a real connector in a relationship. These qualities can set the stage for love to bloom, inspiring valuable ideas and actions, producing creative plans and unique experiences. Also, these qualities give birth to innovative solutions and effective togetherness.

It's clear how loving communication provides you an opportunity to touch your spouse's heart with profound words and ideas. Make a choice now to use the best possible words as you communicate with your spouse. Change the future of your marriage by moving away from damaging forces like power struggles.

~ Make a choice to reject power struggles ~

Choice

14

STANDING IN YOUR OWN WAY

Every individual is responsible
for their own behavior.
~ Melody Beattie

Standing in your own way is a remarkable idea. It gives you a visual picture of how your behavior can affect your movement forward. It's an idea that offers you an opportunity to take a look at your personal actions, choices, and communication. Does this feel challenging? It really isn't. Ask yourself a few questions: "How am I creating problems for myself? How am I contributing to the problems in my marriage? How am I standing in my own way?"

Try to list five things that you know you are doing, which contributes to the problems in your marriage. Be very honest and very sincere; resist the temptation to minimize your negative behaviors. Once your list is complete, write down a list of improvements you can make; then, activate the list by making new choices. This is an inspiring sign of personal growth and progress.

In some instances, when you question yourself, you may not have an answer. In your thoughts, the question doesn't apply to you. It applies to your spouse, because your spouse is responsible for the problems in your marriage. At this point, perhaps, it's time to implement alternate insightful exercise that includes your spouse.

The steps are easy: Ask your spouse to list five things that you can change to improve your marital relationship. At the same time, if your spouse agrees, you can make a list of five things that your spouse could change to improve your relationship. Make sure your list is fair and honest, and does not involve expressions of anger or getting even. To have the best outcome, exchange your lists at the same time.

This is an important moment. Instead of challenging the list, or reacting to the list with anger, or becoming defensive, simply accept the list; allow the list to guide your new positive choices, and enjoy the changes you are creating. Focus your attention on the outcome you want to achieve. It's the most important aspect of this exercise. These ideas will help to change the future of your marriage.

To have an amazing marriage, it is important for you to make a choice to eliminate as many negative actions, reactions, and words as possible. This task is most important to the transformation of your marriage and the enrichment of your future. It provides an opportunity for you and your spouse to restore positive emotions to your marriage, while encouraging your love to sincerely grow.

~ Make a choice to stop standing in your own way ~

Choice

15

WHAT ARE YOU BRINGING TO THE TABLE

Each person is a unique part of life and
here to contribute something.
~ Deepak Chopra

What are you bringing to the table? In other words, what are you bringing to your marriage? Imagine a large table standing in front of you, what are you placing on the table. Make sure that you think of tangible things and intangible things; items you can touch and items you can't touch. Here are a few examples, fun, laughter, love, happiness, peace, attractiveness, passion, money, prestige, social status, knowledge, social friends, travel, communication skills, or harmony.

Take a moment and think of the negatives you're bringing to the table. Make a list of the items you're contributing to your marriage. As you prepare your list, include positive as well as negative contributions to your marriage.

At this point, determine what you're taking from the table. Are you being fair? Are you taking more than you're bringing? Often, one spouse is extremely generous; bringing many things of value to the marriage. The other spouse hardly brings anything to the marriage, but expects a great deal. This type of marriage frequently struggles to survive.

For a spouse to live in a marriage that is consistently unfair puts the marriage at risk. If a spouse brings things of quality to the marriage, and takes things of quality; the marriage advances and love grows. However, if a spouse brings negatives to the table and takes positives away; that spouse sabotages the marriage and their future.

A fantastic objective is to bring the best to the marriage, share the best, and take the best. Some couples realize that as they develop their marriage, their marriage develops them. It is a very unique process with wonderful benefits as long as their contribution is valuable and consistent, offering things of quality, and taking things of quality. Being exceptionally generous, fair, and loving, adds value to your marriage while benefiting you, your spouse, and your future.

~ Make a choice to bring things of value to your marriage ~

PART THREE

DEALING WITH THE PRESENT

Change your thoughts and you
change your world.
~ Norman Vincent Peale

Choice

16

THE REWARD OF CHANGE

The secret of change is to give your total
energy to creating the new, instead
of battling the old.

~ Socrates

Change is exciting, when you can push fear away. As you make new choices, pay attention to how things unfold in your relationship with your spouse. Especially, notice how your feelings adjust to the changes that occur. It's a gradual process, but very inspiring when both spouses have a strong commitment to positive choices and flexibility.

Your personal experience of rewarding changes validates for you that your new progressive decisions have a creative dimension. A transforming quality that has the ability to enhance, improve and dramatically change you, your marriage, and your life. The secret to your success rests with a sincere commitment, enriching choices, and positive consistent effort.

Observe the connection between your personal positive changes and the change that automatically occurs in your marital relationship and marriage itself. That's right. As a couple, your choices of communication and your choices of behavior create your marriage, your marital relationship, your progress, and your future. This is a powerful realization.

As you make personal positive choices, and your spouse makes personal positive choices, your future arrives transformed. That's the power of a choice; an incredible agent of change in your life.

These valuable changes give birth to a deeper more sustained love that provides it's own rewards. Your willingness to welcome a new perspective, grasp new ideas, and implement new choices provides you and your spouse with an opportunity to have the marriage you have envisioned, an amazing marriage.

Keep in mind, negative thinking, negative behavior, and negative feelings may occasionally challenge you. Prevent them from destroying your marriage and your future, by focusing your attention on expressing love. Quite fascinating is the fact that love is the greatest power in the world.

Strive to be amazing in all that you do, it's a way to add excitement to your marriage, your future, and your life.

~ Make a choice to value the change you are creating ~

Choice

17

WIN–WIN DECISIONS

Creative thinking may lead to the awareness
that you can do things a different way.

~ Rudolf Flesch

Decision-making can be an exciting process, a process that a couple loves to participate in throughout their marriage. But, in many marriages trying to make a decision can trigger arguments and conflicts that seem to last forever. Generally, each spouse offers a choice, then battles for their choice. Finally, a decision is achieved by a win-lose method. One spouse's choice is accepted, and the other spouse's choice is rejected. This means when any decision is made one person leaves the discussion feeling disappointed or upset about their loss. This type of exchange seems to have a ripple effect, so that the real loss is in the marriage itself.

In an amazing marriage, couples create win-win solutions. A win-win solution is an inclusive decision. That's right. An inclusive decision means that each spouse receives something of similar value when the decision is made. It's a creative way to solve problems and reach agreements as a married couple. This means that each spouse is pleased with the outcome. This approach is easy and creative; it requires that you quickly shift your focus from the problem to the solution.

To reach a win-win decision: First, each spouse expresses his or her choice. In other words, what he or she truly wants. Next, both spouses turn their attention to an *inclusive* solution, a solution that includes something of value for both spouses.

The easiest way to create an inclusive solution is to think of what your spouse wants or would like. Think in a broad creative way, this process is a type of barter.

At this point, each spouse presents an inclusive offer during a discussion. After considering each offer, the couple selects one offer. No matter which option they select, it is a win–win for the couple. Decision-making becomes a very pleasant aspect of the marriage.

To illustrate how this method works, imagine planning your vacation with your spouse. You express how thrilled you would be to visit Walt Disney World, and your spouse tells you how passionate he is about visiting the Florida Keys.

Immediately, you both turn your attention to creating an inclusive decision to present. During a planning discussion, you both propose your inclusive offer as a possible option.

Your spouse makes the first offer: If you agree to vacation in the Florida Keys, he will extend the vacation three days so the two of you can visit your sister as well. Next, you present your offer: If your spouse agrees to a Disney World vacation, he can plan the next two vacations.

Two great choices, so you flip a coin. It's a win-win decision; you're going to vacation at Disney World and your spouse will select the next two vacations. You're both happy and ready to go on vacation!

~ Make a choice to create win-win decisions ~

Choice

18

BEING A TEAM

*You can achieve something truly valuable with
the cooperation of an unselfish team.*

~ Albert Einstein

Surprisingly, becoming a team in a marriage is one of the most perplexing concepts for most couples. Many couples are unfamiliar with the practice and benefits of teamwork in a marriage. Instead, couples are more familiar with the process and rewards of functioning separately. This way of functioning in a marriage creates unforeseen challenges, when one partner makes decisions and choices their spouse disagrees with strongly.

Major trouble rest at the heart of the marriage, as each spouse tries to maneuver to obtain his or her way, or to be deceptive. Many couples use competition, manipulation, or unproductive behaviors to have things go their way. The marriage becomes more of an invisible chess game, than a truly loving team. All of these behaviors emerge as each spouse tries to stand up for their independence.

Certainly, you can change this pattern, if teamwork is a challenge in your marriage. The easiest way to become a real team in your marriage is for you and your spouse to willingly compromise when necessary. This type of flexibility makes compromise possible. Clearly, this entails more conversations as a couple - not debates, but fact- finding chats. Learning about each other's preferences, making time to discuss when it's best for you and your spouse to share responsibilities. Also, exploring when the two of you can physically accomplish things together, when the two of you can make creative plans, and when you can function independently of each other. This type of communication removes many troubling experiences from the marriage. In this case, practice is certainly the key to success; you learn to work as a team by actively accomplishing things together.

This remarkable way of functioning in your marriage opens you up to fascinating results. This is a bonus for a couple when creative change is welcomed.

Every sincere successful attempt to become a terrific team, propels your intimacy to another level. It's one more dimension of the marriage that brings you fulfillment as a couple and increases the love between you.

~ Make a choice to work as a team ~

Choice

19

EXPECTATIONS

A mindset with positive expectation is the
mark of the superior personality.

~ Brian Tracy

Sharing your expectations with your spouse might be one of the most enlightening experiences you may share. This pivotal event will change things for the better or at best improve them.

No need for guessing, when expectations are expressed, you know exactly what your spouse wants or needs. It's clear to you what your spouse expects from you, from the marriage, and from your future. It makes growing your love easier and more rewarding. Your spouse's most important information is now available to you, to act on when necessary. In the same way, your meaningful information is now available to your spouse. It's like going on a vacation with a map, as oppose to trying to blindly find your way. Plan to talk and share expectations as soon as possible. It's best to write them down.

Of course, discussing what you expect takes time. Start today, be specific and detailed as you express your expectations for your relationship, or your intimacy or your finances or other aspects of your married life.

Listen carefully as your spouse talks, giving your full

attention and thought to the ideas expressed. Ask questions, and explore how you might implement what your spouse expects. Use this time to become enlightened and informed; refrain from judging, criticizing, challenging, or arguing about your spouse's expectations. Listen with your whole heart. Let this favorable experience draw you closer together as a couple.

If an expectation is expressed that you strongly disagree with, see if you and your spouse can compromise and find a fair solution.

One other helpful idea, take time before events or activities to discuss what you're expecting. In this way, if you want to stay later or leave early, it's spelled out before you arrive. If you want to chat with specific people or spend more time with each other, it's clear to both of you how the evening will progress.

An amazing marriage offers you an opportunity to have incredible experiences, and fewer problems. Discussions about your expectations will create trust, contentment, and more joy. This type of harmony will strengthen your love.

~ Make a choice to discuss your expectations ~

Choice

20

A VOLLEY

Communication flows easy and
effectively when trust is high.
~ Stephen Covey

Gratifying conversations with your spouse can stir your
heart and awaken your awareness. Words become treasured
nuggets of thought that broaden your vision, enhance your
understanding, and ignite your aspirations. Conversations
emerge as uniquely meaningful experiences that are eagerly
anticipated and instantly enjoyed by you and your spouse.

A great way to have captivating conversations as a
married couple is to have what I refer to as a *volley*. A *volley*
is a very enjoyable means of communication that only
involves adding ideas. Somewhat like a chain, each idea
becomes a link in the conversation. This type of conversation
inspires the free flow of ideas and creativity. One spouse
speaks, sharing an idea; then the other spouse speaks,
adding an idea. This back and forth exchange continues to
the end of the conversation. This process is comfortable,
exciting, and extremely rewarding.

You can share interesting ideas, spontaneous insights,
creative possibilities, significant experiences, and personal
reflections. Observe how this technique omits criticism,
defensiveness, debates, and arguments. Can you see how

expansive and enriched your thoughts become when you are not encumbered by negative comments or a challenging viewpoint? Opposing, critiquing, and correcting are not a part of what I refer to as a *volley*.

In an amazing marriage, the goal of a conversation is to share, enrich, and enhance. Rewarding conversations create an open and trusting atmosphere that adds excitement to the experience, and value to your marital relationship.

~ Make a choice to use a volley ~

Choice

21

COMMUNICATING FEELINGS

All that you want is right outside
your comfort zone.

~ Robert Allen

In a marriage, the key to successfully discussing hurt feelings starts with organizing your words so you're understood, and then, communicating so you don't offend the listener. The moment you lose sight of these two vital components, useful communication stops, replaced by extremely challenging words, which is the case in many marriages.

Conversations that run into trouble, those that become angry exchanges have the power to sabotage intimacy, love, and trust. Clearly, these conversations move things downhill rapidly. At this point, the relationship needs to be rescued.

Before this happens, try first to put the brakes on unproductive exchanges. It is wise to give some thought to what you're going to say, before you say it. I realize that sharing thoughts openly and freely feels right. However, you can achieve the best outcome if you think about your words before you express them. Especially when discussing a misunderstanding, discussing your dislikes or expressing how hurt you feel. In these scenarios, when you may be upset it's important not to offend the listener. An offended listener generally moves from being receptive to being defensive, if he or she is still listening at all.

In an amazing marriage, couples achieve the best results when thoughts and feelings are aired in "ownership terms." In other words, you own your feelings, instead of blaming them on your spouse. Remember, your feelings are your reaction to your thoughts about an experience or interaction.

A great way to convey your feelings, for example, *"While we were visiting your parents, I felt embarrassed, when you interrupted me."* Presenting your ideas in this way opens the door for concern from your spouse, and hopefully an apology.

However, when you don't own your feelings, and you blame your spouse; it may spark conflict when it's expressed in this manner: *"While we were visiting your parents, you embarrassed me, when you interrupted me."* These words might certainly trigger an angry reply from your spouse or silence. Your hurt feelings may go unaddressed, as you both try to defend your positions.

Communication is an extremely important aspect of your marriage because it helps to develop your relationship as a couple, so make it the best. Convey your feelings and thoughts in ways that help you to receive understanding, support, and a resolution.

~ Make a choice to own your feelings ~

Choice

22

ATTENTION

*I recall everything about you. You're the
person who wasn't paying attention.*
~Suzanne Collins

Attention is an extremely important aspect of a marriage, and it is rarely discussed openly, but carefully monitored by each spouse. In many instances, a spouse feels loved or unloved by the attention or inattention he or she receives. Experiencing attention brightens your heart, and makes you feel valuable and special; however, a consistent lack of attention breaks your heart, and makes you feel rejected and pushed away.

The way many couples have embraced text messaging, cell phones, email, social websites, and Internet browsing has created serious problems in their marriages. These private actions take time away from activities couples normally share. If this is a major problem in your marriage, discuss it with your spouse and develop a specific plan for accessing cellphones and computers when you're together. This frees up time to give each other attention

Of course, partners in a marriage desire various forms of attention. One spouse arrives home, checks to see if his spouse offers him a greeting or a hug. Another spouse, during a conversation watches to see if her spouse is listening.

Attention has become a tool to measure a spouse's commitment. Since a married couple agrees to move through life together, to function together, to be romantically involved, to support one another, and to be personally involved; attention becomes very significant to the life of the relationship and marriage.

In an amazing marriage, the couple strives not only to give attention, but to provide their spouse with quality attention. Certainly, you may ask yourself in practical terms, what does this mean? It means you are fully present, fully participating, and fully contributing as you interact with your spouse, bringing quality to your shared experience.

Moreover, it's reassuring to your spouse to know that when you show up, quality attention shows up, and meaningful interaction shows up. Your marriage becomes more gratifying, as you and your spouse provide enriching attention to each other; the value of your shared experiences increase significantly. This is an exciting reality. As the attention you receive from your spouse becomes more enriching, the more gratifying your marriage becomes to you. Resulting in both spouses feeling loved and treasured.

~ Make a choice to give your spouse quality attention ~

Choice

23

FEELING LIKE A WINNER

The person who brings forth the best in me,
becomes my best friend.
~ Henry Ford

One extraordinary feature of having an amazing marriage is the ability of a couple to inspire each other to feel like a winner. To encounter this kind of unique support, gives wings to your spirit, and vision to your life. Most spouses rarely experience this form of love and encouragement; but when they do, it can elevate their self-esteem, inspire accomplishments, broaden their goals, and deepen their love – moving a spouse to a whole new amazing level.

As you travel through life with your spouse, it's important to realize, the more positives you pour into your relationship the more it enhances you both. The more positives you pour into each other, the more enriched the marriage becomes. Every aspect of your marriage benefits when you and your spouse decide to make each other feel like winners.

If you feel yourself resisting this concept, if this concept is difficult to grasp; negative thinking may be the problem. Remember, negative thoughts lead to maintaining a pessimistic perspective, drawing opposing conclusions, making undesirable remarks, and creating unhelpful reactions. If this is the case for you, work diligently to make a choice to embrace a positive perspective and treat your spouse like a winner.

Imagine giving your spouse the gift of feeling like a winner, or a hero, or a success; then, envision your spouse giving you the same special gift. This priceless gem will bring out the best in you and your spouse; pouring love into your marriage, and enthusiasm into your spirit. Love combined with amazing support can help you and your spouse experience what appears to be the miraculous.

~ Make a choice to help your spouse feel like a winner ~

Choice

24

FUN AND BOREDOM

People seldom succeed unless they have
fun with what they're doing.
~ Dale Carnegie

Having fun with your spouse is an incredible way to share
your time together. Laughter awakens a special kind of joy in
a marriage and play ignites the best kind of fun for a couple.
Two most important keys to a long-term marriage are to
keep the fun and laughter alive and consistent in your
marriage, inviting and creating new joy filled experiences.

You may have discovered this fact. Boredom is the enemy
of a marriage. It numbs your spirit, dries up the love
between the two partners, and in time becomes unbearable.
Boredom damages marital relationships by impacting the
couple emotionally in a negative way. It's correct to assert
that boredom drains the life out of a marriage.

Watch for signs of boredom in your marriage. Boredom
springs up in the marriage after complacency takes over.
First, there is the feeling of happiness or contentment. You
and your spouse become at ease with a specific daily routine.
A sense of pleasure may fill your marriage, without realizing
it, you start giving less effort and change to your marital
relationship since things are going well. Soon boredom moves
in and quietly drains your energy and joy.

No one wants a future without change, hope, or new activities. Boredom has away of robbing you of your time. Stop this from occurring in your marriage; make fun plans, add excitement and joy to your date-nights, and create lovely romantic evenings.

Keep your marriage full of laughter and fun. Make sure that you play together and enjoy surprises. Include friends as you add new exciting experiences and enjoyable fun activities to your marriage.

Plan your date-nights so they are fun and unforgettable; start today. Try some pleasurable activities that you might be experiencing for the first time, such as dancing, swimming, horseback riding, chess, golf, tennis, or weekend trips - you have the idea. Make your marriage an exciting adventure. It is one way to strengthen your love and deepen your marital bond. (*Also, look over the resources in the back of the book for new amazing places and extraordinary experiences to try.*)

~ Make a choice to play and have fun with your spouse ~

Choice

25

LOVE AND MARRIAGE

If you are loved; then love and be lovable.
~ Benjamin Franklin

Love inspires the human heart and brings individuals together in remarkable ways. It's a real mystery how love emerges. Love seems to appear unexpectedly when couples are dating, bringing with it excitement, joy, laughter, and many other delightful emotions. Yet, once love is actively a part of a relationship, and the engagement and wedding are over, another surprising unexpected thing happens.

The love shared by the married couple becomes their responsibility to keep alive, nurture, sustain, and cherish. Surprisingly, many couples are unaware of this incredible unforeseen assignment and responsibility when they fall in love.

Frequently, movies and love songs often give the impression that love sustains itself. Somehow, love is expected to keep itself alive and dynamic throughout the marriage or a relationship. At first, the idea may seem romantic; with a closer look, it's clear this idea can create misleading expectations and unforeseen disappointment for a couple.

Love is a living thing; to grow and survive in a marriage, love needs to be continuously nurtured, refreshed, and improved.

It's the couple's unique task to nurture their love with words and actions that are filled with qualities such as joy, hope, kindness, humor, happiness, sincerity, harmony, forgiveness, consideration, honesty, fairness, appreciation, affection, beauty, generosity, intimacy, trust, patience, and dedication.

As the couple nurtures their love, each spouse is being transformed as well as the marriage. If a couple wants a love forever, an enduring love, it's their task to cultivate the highest positive qualities and nurture each other with them. By doing so, the love between them will grow and deepen.

However, if negative energy, words, and actions occupy the marriage; love will vanish just as mysteriously as it arrived. Constant hurtful conflict, expressions of un-forgiveness, anger, insincere apologies, inconsideration, deception, excuses, and dishonesty; quickly extinguish love.

For this reason, make sure that you embrace love with your whole heart, mind, actions, and words. Sustain your love by consistently putting loving qualities into practice. Give your time and best efforts to letting your spouse know the extent and depth of your love by your actions and reactions. Make love welcomed in your marriage, remember that your words and actions can invite love to stay forever.

~ Make a choice to be loveable and loving ~

Choice

26

LOVE AND INTIMACY

*People who have never experienced the deep intimacy
and intense companionship of joyful mutual love
have missed the best that life has to offer.*
~Bertrand Russell

Once the heart feels love, the human spirit seems to secretly long for intimacy. Affectionate closeness, trusting nearness, helps to connect people who care about one another in a significant way.

When intimacy progresses and develops in a marital relationship, it's not unusual for a couple to experience an exciting gratifying pleasure in all the dimensions of their marriage. The partners are able to enjoy each other in new, expansive, exhilarating ways. In other words, two people together create incredible experiences greater than they could have created alone. This type of remarkable compatibility creates exceptional expressions of love.

Once a married couple reaches this level of enjoyable compatibility; their sexual relationship and physical desire become intensely gratifying. Their love, oneness, trust, and thoughtfulness allow them to experience a fantastic physical expression of love on a sexual level that surpasses their expectations.

But, it's quite different for many partners in a marriage.

Some couples are unable to obtain an incredible happiness and exciting intimacy because negative words, actions, and thoughts block and impede their progress. You know, anger, conflict, getting even, un-forgiveness, dishonesty, stubborn resistance, and the list marches on. These negatives strip away love and intimacy, replacing it with hurt feelings and resentments. Without realizing it, these spouses allow their negative words and offensive actions to rob them of amazing love and exciting affectionate closeness.

Your choices are the change agents in your life, spend time today, considering new choices that will develop and protect your intimacy. Keeping in mind that you live in your marriage, and you spend your life in your marriage; for this significant reason, make it amazing.

~ Make a choice to grow and develop your intimacy ~

Choice

27

CREATING AN AMAZING MARRIAGE

It has come to my attention that those who are successful
rarely sat back and let things happen to them.
They went out and happened to things.
~ Leonardo da Vinci

Creating an amazing marriage is an exciting adventure. It means experiencing a new type of marriage, a marriage that focuses on creating unforgettable experiences and wonderful memories. Not arguments, opposition, and selfish pursuits that may lead to divorce, but a marital relationship that is genuinely fulfilling, and terrifically gratifying in each aspect of the marriage, makes it an amazing marriage.

The best way to get started is to understand that you are creating your marriage. With your choices and time, you are always creating. However, now you are going to thoughtfully and creatively produce specific new and rewarding experiences for your day, your week, and your month. Giving your energy to creative planning and exciting implementation. Creating amazing experiences will offer your marriage new enjoyment and happiness.

This means designing events in your day with a vision of the big picture as well as an attention to details. With a notebook and pen, start listing ideas for enhancing daily plans and experiences. Each day, refine your ideas. Keep in mind that surprises are a big hit with most spouses.

Creativity makes a marriage a great place to live in, love in and grow in. A great way to put your love, your intimacy, your relationship, and your experiences on a higher level is to use creative ideas.

As a couple, when you develop extraordinary plans and activate incredible details, you are not only experiencing something new and different, you are creating wonderful memories. Once you start making creative plans, wonderful ideas may come to mind, you can make events and situations more interesting, more enjoyable, and more captivating. This eliminates boredom, the real enemy of a marriage.

One of the best surprises when creating an amazing marriage is the awareness of growing as a person. It makes you more exciting, more interesting, and more lovable. Creating an amazing marriage is one way for a couple to embrace a rewarding life.

Remember, with your choices, you are always creating. By creating an amazing marriage, you are electing to experience positive extraordinary events and terrific memories. Instead of devoting your energy and effort to conflict, anger, resentment, and stubborn opposition; make a choice to embrace love and creative planning. Fill your life with exciting change and valuable memories.

Focus your energy, effort, and attention on creating a marriage that you can live-in, love-in, grow-in, and enjoy. Have an incredible life, an amazing marriage, and a love forever.

~ Make a choice to have an amazing marriage ~

AFTERWORD

A Love Forever was written with married couples in mind. More specifically, couples who are teachable and motivated to implement new choices. For these couples, it was my passion to write a concise practical book that each spouse could use individually and actively.

It was my hope that each couple might experience first hand how their choices are the real change agents in their lives. With their creative choices, they can produce the best possible marriage. A marriage filled with enjoyable experiences, rewarding interactions, great conversations, incredible intimacy, as well as a growing and enduring love.

Although, I cannot guarantee success to anyone, the specific knowledge in this book has proven extremely helpful to married couples over the years.

I'm delighted to share these ideas with you. And, I'm very happy for your progress and the positive changes in your marriage.

If you enjoy learning, I'm happy to invite you to visit MarriageAmazing.com for training, conferences, videos, and much more.

God's blessings,

Lynne

RESOURCE

MEASURING YOUR PROGRESS
Worksheets

*Blessed is the person who finds
wisdom, the person who
gains understanding.*
~ Proverbs 3:13 (NIV)

Problems signal that a change is needed.

PROBLEMS

Measuring Your Progress

It's rewarding to observe positive change. Measure your weekly progress as a *problem solver* below by circling the number that represents your level of progress.

1) No Progress 0 1 2 3 4 5 6 7 8 9 10 Progress

2) No Progress 0 1 2 3 4 5 6 7 8 9 10 Progress

3) No Progress 0 1 2 3 4 5 6 7 8 9 10 Progress

4) No Progress 0 1 2 3 4 5 6 7 8 9 10 Progress

5) No Progress 0 1 2 3 4 5 6 7 8 9 10 Progress

6) No Progress 0 1 2 3 4 5 6 7 8 9 10 Progress

7) No Progress 0 1 2 3 4 5 6 7 8 9 10 Progress

8) No Progress 0 1 2 3 4 5 6 7 8 9 10 Progress

9) No Progress 0 1 2 3 4 5 6 7 8 9 10 Progress

10) No Progress 0 1 2 3 4 5 6 7 8 9 10 Progress

Prevent anger from making decisions for you.

REMOVING ANGER
Measuring Your Progress

It's rewarding to observe positive change. Measure your weekly progress with *removing anger* by circling the number that represents your level of progress.

1) No Progress 0 1 2 3 4 5 6 7 8 9 10 Progress

2) No Progress 0 1 2 3 4 5 6 7 8 9 10 Progress

3) No Progress 0 1 2 3 4 5 6 7 8 9 10 Progress

4) No Progress 0 1 2 3 4 5 6 7 8 9 10 Progress

5) No Progress 0 1 2 3 4 5 6 7 8 9 10 Progress

6) No Progress 0 1 2 3 4 5 6 7 8 9 10 Progress

7) No Progress 0 1 2 3 4 5 6 7 8 9 10 Progress

8) No Progress 0 1 2 3 4 5 6 7 8 9 10 Progress

9) No Progress 0 1 2 3 4 5 6 7 8 9 10 Progress

10) No Progress 0 1 2 3 4 5 6 7 8 9 10 Progress

Forgiveness clears the way for love.

LET IT GO

Measuring Your Progress

It's rewarding to observe positive change. Measure your weekly progress with *forgiveness* by circling the number that represents your level of progress.

1) No Progress   0 1 2 3 4 5 6 7 8 9 10   Progress

2) No Progress   0 1 2 3 4 5 6 7 8 9 10   Progress

3) No Progress   0 1 2 3 4 5 6 7 8 9 10   Progress

4) No Progress   0 1 2 3 4 5 6 7 8 9 10   Progress

5) No Progress   0 1 2 3 4 5 6 7 8 9 10   Progress

6) No Progress   0 1 2 3 4 5 6 7 8 9 10   Progress

7) No Progress   0 1 2 3 4 5 6 7 8 9 10   Progress

8) No Progress   0 1 2 3 4 5 6 7 8 9 10   Progress

9) No Progress   0 1 2 3 4 5 6 7 8 9 10   Progress

10) No Progress   0 1 2 3 4 5 6 7 8 9 10   Progress

*An apology can breathe new
life into a marriage.*

APOLOGIZING
Measuring Your Progress

It's rewarding to observe positive change. Measure your weekly progress with *apologies* by circling the number that represents your level of progress.

1) No Progress 0 1 2 3 4 5 6 7 8 9 10 Progress

2) No Progress 0 1 2 3 4 5 6 7 8 9 10 Progress

3) No Progress 0 1 2 3 4 5 6 7 8 9 10 Progress

4) No Progress 0 1 2 3 4 5 6 7 8 9 10 Progress

5) No Progress 0 1 2 3 4 5 6 7 8 9 10 Progress

6) No Progress 0 1 2 3 4 5 6 7 8 9 10 Progress

7) No Progress 0 1 2 3 4 5 6 7 8 9 10 Progress

8) No Progress 0 1 2 3 4 5 6 7 8 9 10 Progress

9) No Progress 0 1 2 3 4 5 6 7 8 9 10 Progress

10) No Progress 0 1 2 3 4 5 6 7 8 9 10 Progress

*Assumptions play a huge part in the
misunderstandings and arguments
in a marriage.*

MAKING
ASSUMPTIONS

Measuring Your Progress

It's rewarding to observe positive change. Measure your weekly progress with *omitting assumptions,* by circling the number that represents your level of progress.

1) No Progress 0 1 2 3 4 5 6 7 8 9 10 Progress

2) No Progress 0 1 2 3 4 5 6 7 8 9 10 Progress

3) No Progress 0 1 2 3 4 5 6 7 8 9 10 Progress

4) No Progress 0 1 2 3 4 5 6 7 8 9 10 Progress

5) No Progress 0 1 2 3 4 5 6 7 8 9 10 Progress

6) No Progress 0 1 2 3 4 5 6 7 8 9 10 Progress

7) No Progress 0 1 2 3 4 5 6 7 8 9 10 Progress

8) No Progress 0 1 2 3 4 5 6 7 8 9 10 Progress

9) No Progress 0 1 2 3 4 5 6 7 8 9 10 Progress

10) No Progress 0 1 2 3 4 5 6 7 8 9 10 Progress

Conflict is not an answer. Love is the solution.

CONFLICT

Measuring Your Progress

It's rewarding to observe positive change. Measure your weekly progress with *removing conflict*, by circling the number that represents your level of progress.

1) No Progress   0 1 2 3 4 5 6 7 8 9 10   Progress

2) No Progress   0 1 2 3 4 5 6 7 8 9 10   Progress

3) No Progress   0 1 2 3 4 5 6 7 8 9 10   Progress

4) No Progress   0 1 2 3 4 5 6 7 8 9 10   Progress

5) No Progress   0 1 2 3 4 5 6 7 8 9 10   Progress

6) No Progress   0 1 2 3 4 5 6 7 8 9 10   Progress

7) No Progress   0 1 2 3 4 5 6 7 8 9 10   Progress

8) No Progress   0 1 2 3 4 5 6 7 8 9 10   Progress

9) No Progress   0 1 2 3 4 5 6 7 8 9 10   Progress

10) No Progress   0 1 2 3 4 5 6 7 8 9 10   Progress

Power- struggles breakdown trust in a marriage.

POWER
STRUGGLES

Measuring Your Progress

It's rewarding to observe positive change. Measure your weekly progress with *power struggles,* by circling the number that represents your level of progress.

1) No Progress 0 1 2 3 4 5 6 7 8 9 10 Progress

2) No Progress 0 1 2 3 4 5 6 7 8 9 10 Progress

3) No Progress 0 1 2 3 4 5 6 7 8 9 10 Progress

4) No Progress 0 1 2 3 4 5 6 7 8 9 10 Progress

5) No Progress 0 1 2 3 4 5 6 7 8 9 10 Progress

6) No Progress 0 1 2 3 4 5 6 7 8 9 10 Progress

7) No Progress 0 1 2 3 4 5 6 7 8 9 10 Progress

8) No Progress 0 1 2 3 4 5 6 7 8 9 10 Progress

9) No Progress 0 1 2 3 4 5 6 7 8 9 10 Progress

10) No Progress 0 1 2 3 4 5 6 7 8 9 10 Progress

Words and actions develop or destroy a marriage.

CRITICISM

Measuring Your Progress

It's rewarding to observe positive change. Measure your weekly progress with *removing criticism*, by circling the number that represents your level of progress.

1) No Progress   0 1 2 3 4 5 6 7 8 9 10   Progress

2) No Progress   0 1 2 3 4 5 6 7 8 9 10   Progress

3) No Progress   0 1 2 3 4 5 6 7 8 9 10   Progress

4) No Progress   0 1 2 3 4 5 6 7 8 9 10   Progress

5) No Progress   0 1 2 3 4 5 6 7 8 9 10   Progress

6) No Progress   0 1 2 3 4 5 6 7 8 9 10   Progress

7) No Progress   0 1 2 3 4 5 6 7 8 9 10   Progress

8) No Progress   0 1 2 3 4 5 6 7 8 9 10   Progress

9) No Progress   0 1 2 3 4 5 6 7 8 9 10   Progress

10) No Progress   0 1 2 3 4 5 6 7 8 9 10   Progress

Examine your thoughts,
actions, and words.

STANDING IN YOUR OWN WAY
Measuring Your Progress

It's rewarding to observe positive change. Measure your weekly progress with *self-discovery* by circling the number that represents your level of progress.

1) No Progress 0 1 2 3 4 5 6 7 8 9 10 Progress

2) No Progress 0 1 2 3 4 5 6 7 8 9 10 Progress

3) No Progress 0 1 2 3 4 5 6 7 8 9 10 Progress

4) No Progress 0 1 2 3 4 5 6 7 8 9 10 Progress

5) No Progress 0 1 2 3 4 5 6 7 8 9 10 Progress

6) No Progress 0 1 2 3 4 5 6 7 8 9 10 Progress

7) No Progress 0 1 2 3 4 5 6 7 8 9 10 Progress

8) No Progress 0 1 2 3 4 5 6 7 8 9 10 Progress

9) No Progress 0 1 2 3 4 5 6 7 8 9 10 Progress

10) No Progress 0 1 2 3 4 5 6 7 8 9 10 Progress

Contribute something of value
to your marriage.

WHAT ARE YOU BRINGING
TO THE TABLE
Measuring Your Progress

It's rewarding to observe positive change. Measure your weekly progress with *contributing something of value to your marriage* by circling the number that represents your level of progress.

1) No Progress 0 1 2 3 4 5 6 7 8 9 10 Progress

2) No Progress 0 1 2 3 4 5 6 7 8 9 10 Progress

3) No Progress 0 1 2 3 4 5 6 7 8 9 10 Progress

4) No Progress 0 1 2 3 4 5 6 7 8 9 10 Progress

5) No Progress 0 1 2 3 4 5 6 7 8 9 10 Progress

6) No Progress 0 1 2 3 4 5 6 7 8 9 10 Progress

7) No Progress 0 1 2 3 4 5 6 7 8 9 10 Progress

8) No Progress 0 1 2 3 4 5 6 7 8 9 10 Progress

9) No Progress 0 1 2 3 4 5 6 7 8 9 10 Progress

10) No Progress 0 1 2 3 4 5 6 7 8 9 10 Progress

*New choices and new outcomes
are exciting.*

THE REWARD OF CHANGE
Measuring Your Progress

It's rewarding to observe positive change. Measure your weekly progress with *implementing change* by circling the number that represents your level of progress.

1) No Progress 0 1 2 3 4 5 6 7 8 9 10 Progress

2) No Progress 0 1 2 3 4 5 6 7 8 9 10 Progress

3) No Progress 0 1 2 3 4 5 6 7 8 9 10 Progress

4) No Progress 0 1 2 3 4 5 6 7 8 9 10 Progress

5) No Progress 0 1 2 3 4 5 6 7 8 9 10 Progress

6) No Progress 0 1 2 3 4 5 6 7 8 9 10 Progress

7) No Progress 0 1 2 3 4 5 6 7 8 9 10 Progress

8) No Progress 0 1 2 3 4 5 6 7 8 9 10 Progress

9) No Progress 0 1 2 3 4 5 6 7 8 9 10 Progress

10) No Progress 0 1 2 3 4 5 6 7 8 9 10 Progress

Working as a team means making
inclusive decisions.

BEING A TEAM
Measuring Your Progress

It's rewarding to observe positive change. Measure your weekly progress with *teamwork* by circling the number that represents your level of progress.

1) No Progress 0 1 2 3 4 5 6 7 8 9 10 Progress

2) No Progress 0 1 2 3 4 5 6 7 8 9 10 Progress

3) No Progress 0 1 2 3 4 5 6 7 8 9 10 Progress

4) No Progress 0 1 2 3 4 5 6 7 8 9 10 Progress

5) No Progress 0 1 2 3 4 5 6 7 8 9 10 Progress

6) No Progress 0 1 2 3 4 5 6 7 8 9 10 Progress

7) No Progress 0 1 2 3 4 5 6 7 8 9 10 Progress

8) No Progress 0 1 2 3 4 5 6 7 8 9 10 Progress

9) No Progress 0 1 2 3 4 5 6 7 8 9 10 Progress

10) No Progress 0 1 2 3 4 5 6 7 8 9 10 Progress

Sharing your expectations, prepares you for enjoyable experiences.

EXPECTATIONS
Measuring Your Progress

It's rewarding to observe positive change. Measure your weekly progress with *discussing expectations* by circling the number that represents your level of progress.

1) No Progress 0 1 2 3 4 5 6 7 8 9 10 Progress

2) No Progress 0 1 2 3 4 5 6 7 8 9 10 Progress

3) No Progress 0 1 2 3 4 5 6 7 8 9 10 Progress

4) No Progress 0 1 2 3 4 5 6 7 8 9 10 Progress

5) No Progress 0 1 2 3 4 5 6 7 8 9 10 Progress

6) No Progress 0 1 2 3 4 5 6 7 8 9 10 Progress

7) No Progress 0 1 2 3 4 5 6 7 8 9 10 Progress

8) No Progress 0 1 2 3 4 5 6 7 8 9 10 Progress

9) No Progress 0 1 2 3 4 5 6 7 8 9 10 Progress

10) No Progress 0 1 2 3 4 5 6 7 8 9 10 Progress

Interesting conversations enhance a marriage.

A VOLLEY
Measuring Your Progress

It's rewarding to observe positive change. Measure your weekly progress with *communication* by circling the number that represents your level of progress.

1) No Progress   0 1 2 3 4 5 6 7 8 9 10   Progress

2) No Progress   0 1 2 3 4 5 6 7 8 9 10   Progress

3) No Progress   0 1 2 3 4 5 6 7 8 9 10   Progress

4) No Progress   0 1 2 3 4 5 6 7 8 9 10   Progress

5) No Progress   0 1 2 3 4 5 6 7 8 9 10   Progress

6) No Progress   0 1 2 3 4 5 6 7 8 9 10   Progress

7) No Progress   0 1 2 3 4 5 6 7 8 9 10   Progress

8) No Progress   0 1 2 3 4 5 6 7 8 9 10   Progress

9) No Progress   0 1 2 3 4 5 6 7 8 9 10   Progress

10) No Progress   0 1 2 3 4 5 6 7 8 9 10   Progress

WIN-WIN choices lead to win-win solutions.

WIN-WIN DECISIONS
Measuring Your Progress

It's rewarding to observe positive change. Measure your weekly progress with *Win-Win decisions* by circling the number that represents your level of progress.

1) No Progress 0 1 2 3 4 5 6 7 8 9 10 Progress

2) No Progress 0 1 2 3 4 5 6 7 8 9 10 Progress

3) No Progress 0 1 2 3 4 5 6 7 8 9 10 Progress

4) No Progress 0 1 2 3 4 5 6 7 8 9 10 Progress

5) No Progress 0 1 2 3 4 5 6 7 8 9 10 Progress

6) No Progress 0 1 2 3 4 5 6 7 8 9 10 Progress

7) No Progress 0 1 2 3 4 5 6 7 8 9 10 Progress

8) No Progress 0 1 2 3 4 5 6 7 8 9 10 Progress

9) No Progress 0 1 2 3 4 5 6 7 8 9 10 Progress

10) No Progress 0 1 2 3 4 5 6 7 8 9 10 Progress

For the best results, own your true feelings.

DISCUSSING FEELINGS
Measuring Your Progress

It's rewarding to observe positive change. Measure your weekly progress with *discussing feelings* by circling the number that represents your level of progress.

1) No Progress 0 1 2 3 4 5 6 7 8 9 10 Progress

2) No Progress 0 1 2 3 4 5 6 7 8 9 10 Progress

3) No Progress 0 1 2 3 4 5 6 7 8 9 10 Progress

4) No Progress 0 1 2 3 4 5 6 7 8 9 10 Progress

5) No Progress 0 1 2 3 4 5 6 7 8 9 10 Progress

6) No Progress 0 1 2 3 4 5 6 7 8 9 10 Progress

7) No Progress 0 1 2 3 4 5 6 7 8 9 10 Progress

8) No Progress 0 1 2 3 4 5 6 7 8 9 10 Progress

9) No Progress 0 1 2 3 4 5 6 7 8 9 10 Progress

10) No Progress 0 1 2 3 4 5 6 7 8 9 10 Progress

*Giving attention to your spouse makes
your spouse feel valued.*

ATTENTION

Measuring Your Progress

It's rewarding to observe positive change. Measure your weekly progress with *giving attention to your spouse* by circling the number that represents your level of progress.

1) No Progress   0 1 2 3 4 5 6 7 8 9 10   Progress

2) No Progress   0 1 2 3 4 5 6 7 8 9 10   Progress

3) No Progress   0 1 2 3 4 5 6 7 8 9 10   Progress

4) No Progress   0 1 2 3 4 5 6 7 8 9 10   Progress

5) No Progress   0 1 2 3 4 5 6 7 8 9 10   Progress

6) No Progress   0 1 2 3 4 5 6 7 8 9 10   Progress

7) No Progress   0 1 2 3 4 5 6 7 8 9 10   Progress

8) No Progress   0 1 2 3 4 5 6 7 8 9 10   Progress

9) No Progress   0 1 2 3 4 5 6 7 8 9 10   Progress

10) No Progress   0 1 2 3 4 5 6 7 8 9 10   Progress

Show your love by giving incredible
support and encouragement.

FEELING LIKE A
WINNER
Measuring Your Progress

It's rewarding to observe positive change. Measure your weekly progress with *making your spouse feel like a winner,* by circling the number that represents your level of progress.

1) No Progress 0 1 2 3 4 5 6 7 8 9 10 Progress

2) No Progress 0 1 2 3 4 5 6 7 8 9 10 Progress

3) No Progress 0 1 2 3 4 5 6 7 8 9 10 Progress

4) No Progress 0 1 2 3 4 5 6 7 8 9 10 Progress

5) No Progress 0 1 2 3 4 5 6 7 8 9 10 Progress

6) No Progress 0 1 2 3 4 5 6 7 8 9 10 Progress

7) No Progress 0 1 2 3 4 5 6 7 8 9 10 Progress

8) No Progress 0 1 2 3 4 5 6 7 8 9 10 Progress

9) No Progress 0 1 2 3 4 5 6 7 8 9 10 Progress

10) No Progress 0 1 2 3 4 5 6 7 8 9 10 Progress

Having fun with your spouse is a terrific kind of joy.

FUN AND BOREDOM

Measuring Your Progress

It's rewarding to observe positive change. Measure your weekly progress with *having fun with your spouse,* by circling the number that represents your level of progress.

1) No Progress 0 1 2 3 4 5 6 7 8 9 10 Progress

2) No Progress 0 1 2 3 4 5 6 7 8 9 10 Progress

3) No Progress 0 1 2 3 4 5 6 7 8 9 10 Progress

4) No Progress 0 1 2 3 4 5 6 7 8 9 10 Progress

5) No Progress 0 1 2 3 4 5 6 7 8 9 10 Progress

6) No Progress 0 1 2 3 4 5 6 7 8 9 10 Progress

7) No Progress 0 1 2 3 4 5 6 7 8 9 10 Progress

8) No Progress 0 1 2 3 4 5 6 7 8 9 10 Progress

9) No Progress 0 1 2 3 4 5 6 7 8 9 10 Progress

10) No Progress 0 1 2 3 4 5 6 7 8 9 10 Progress

*Sustain your love by fantastic
acts of kindness.*

LOVE AND MARRIAGE

Measuring Your Progress

It's rewarding to observe positive change. Measure your weekly progress with *sustaining your love,* by circling the number that represents your level of progress.

1) No Progress 0 1 2 3 4 5 6 7 8 9 10 Progress

2) No Progress 0 1 2 3 4 5 6 7 8 9 10 Progress

3) No Progress 0 1 2 3 4 5 6 7 8 9 10 Progress

4) No Progress 0 1 2 3 4 5 6 7 8 9 10 Progress

5) No Progress 0 1 2 3 4 5 6 7 8 9 10 Progress

6) No Progress 0 1 2 3 4 5 6 7 8 9 10 Progress

7) No Progress 0 1 2 3 4 5 6 7 8 9 10 Progress

8) No Progress 0 1 2 3 4 5 6 7 8 9 10 Progress

9) No Progress 0 1 2 3 4 5 6 7 8 9 10 Progress

10) No Progress 0 1 2 3 4 5 6 7 8 9 10 Progress

*The key to an amazing marriage is
creating fantastic experiences
and wonderful memories.*

AN AMAZING MARRIAGE

Measuring Your Progress

It's rewarding to observe positive change. Measure your weekly progress with *creating an amazing marriage,* by circling the number that represents your level of progress.

1) No Progress 0 1 2 3 4 5 6 7 8 9 10 Progress

2) No Progress 0 1 2 3 4 5 6 7 8 9 10 Progress

3) No Progress 0 1 2 3 4 5 6 7 8 9 10 Progress

4) No Progress 0 1 2 3 4 5 6 7 8 9 10 Progress

5) No Progress 0 1 2 3 4 5 6 7 8 9 10 Progress

6) No Progress 0 1 2 3 4 5 6 7 8 9 10 Progress

7) No Progress 0 1 2 3 4 5 6 7 8 9 10 Progress

8) No Progress 0 1 2 3 4 5 6 7 8 9 10 Progress

9) No Progress 0 1 2 3 4 5 6 7 8 9 10 Progress

10) No Progress 0 1 2 3 4 5 6 7 8 9 10 Progress

RESOURCE

WORKING THINGS OUT

Identifying Problems
Understanding Your Issues
Implementing Solutions

Working Things Out
Specific Problems

The interaction and communication between two spouses create the marital relationship.

In order to improve your marriage each spouse must identify the major problems in the marriage from his or her point of view. It is also important to identify the part he or she is contributing to each problem. As each spouse makes positive changes with his or her choices, the marriage is altered and their problems are altered.

Please identify and list your concerns and problems in the marriage from your point of view.

List your problems or concerns:

1. _____

2. _____

3. _____

4. _____

5. _____

*Successful problem solving brings
happiness and fulfillment to a marriage.*

Working Things Out

Clarifying Your Problems

1. PROBLEM: _____
   What caused this problem?
   How are you contributing to this problem? Why?
   What positive choices can you make to improve this problem?

2. PROBLEM: _____
   What caused this problem?
   How are you contributing to this problem? Why?
   What positive choices can you make to improve this problem?

3. PROBLEM: _____
   What caused this problem?
   How are you contributing to this problem? Why?
   What positive choices can you make to improve this problem?

4. PROBLEM: _____
   What caused this problem?
   How are you contributing to this problem? Why?
   What positive choices can you make to improve this problem?

Each new day brings with it new strength and new ideas.
~ Eleanor Roosevelt

Problem - Solution

Working Things Out

PROBLEM: (Briefly, what is the problem?)_____

_____

SOLUTION: (What solution do you want?)_____

_____

List the steps necessary to achieve your solution.

Step 1 _____

Step 2 _____

Step 3 _____

Step 4 _____

Step 5 _____

Now, implement each step.

RESOURCE

FANTASTIC PLACES
SPECTACULAR EXPERIENCES

*"Write it on your heart that every day is
the best day of your life. You are rich
when you can own the day."*
~ Ralph Waldo Emerson

MAGNIFICENT ROMANTIC WEEKEND

To Consider

THE RITZ-CARLTON, DALLAS
2121 McKinney Avenue
Dallas, Texas 75201
(214) 922-0200

"THE PRINCE CHARMING EXPERIENCE"

CHEYENNE MOUNTAIN RESORT
3225 Broadmoor Valley Road
Colorado Springs, CO 80906
(719) 538-4000

"ROMANCE PACKAGE"

FOUR SEASONS HOTEL, BOSTON
200 Boylston Street
Boston, Massachusetts 02116
(617) 338-4400

"ROMANTIC GETAWAY PACKAGE"

ELEGANT MANSION HOTELS

To Consider

WENTWORTH MANSION

149 – Wentworth Street

Charleston, South Carolina 29401

(888) 466-1886

"NIGHT OF ROMANCE"

WEDMORE PLACE

5810 – Wessex Hundred

Williamsburg, Virginia 23185

(866) 933-6673

"WEDMORE ROMANCE PACKAGE"

SARATOGA ARMS

497 - Broadway

Saratoga Springs, New York 12866

(518) 584-1775

"ROMANTIC ENHANCEMENT PACKAGE"

SPECTACULAR RESTAURANTS

To Consider

TRUE FOOD KITCHEN
Scottsdale Quarter
15191 – N. Scottsdale Rd.
Scottsdale, Arizona 85254
(480) 265-4500

SAISON
178 Townsend Street
San Francisco, CA 94107
(415) 828 7990

THE FRENCH LAUNDRY
6640 Washington Street
Yountville, CA, 94599
(707) 944-2380

LUXURY INNS

To Consider

CASA GRANDVIEW HISTORIC LUXURY INN

1410 - Georgia Avenue
West Palm Beach, Florida 33401
(561) 655-8932

MILLIKEN CREEK INN & SPA

1815 - Silverado Trail
Napa, California 94558
(707) 255-1197

UNION STREET INN

7 - Union Street
Nantucket, Massachusetts 02554
(508) 228-9222

REMARKABLE LODGES
To Consider

BIG CEDAR LODGE
612-Devil's Pool Road
Ridgedale, Missouri 65739
(417) 335-2777

THE LODGE AT WOOD LOCH
109 – River Birch lane
Hawley, Pennsylvania 18428
(570) 685-8500

GLEN LAUREL
14940 – Mt. Olive Road
Rockbridge, Ohio 43149-9736
(740) 385-4070

INCREDIBLE RESTAURANTS
WITH A LOVELY VIEW

To Consider

CALIS
2576 - Aurora Avenue North
Seattle, Washington 98109
(206) 283-3313

ELEMENTS RESTAURANT
(Sanctuary Resort)
5700 - East McDonald Drive
Scottsdale, Arizona 85253
(855) 245-2051

THE RIVER CAFE
One Water Street
Brooklyn, New York 11201
(718) 522-5200

ROMANTIC HOUSEBOAT VACATION

To Consider

LUXURY HOUSEBOAT RENTAL
KEY WEST HARBOR

6000 Peninsular Avenue (Slip 25)
Key West, Florida 33040
(215) 859-7927

PORTLAND OREGON HOUSE
BOAT RENTALS

903 South Mcloughlin Blvd.
Oregon City, Oregon 97045
(503) 656 3132

ROBINHOOD MARINE CENTER

340 – Robin Hood Road
Georgetown, Maine 04548
(800) 255-5206

FANTASTIC ENJOYABLE ISLANDS

To Consider

MACKINAC ISLAND

Tourism Bureau
7274 – Main Street
Mackinac Island, Michigan 49757
(906) 847-3783

SAN JUAN ISLAND

Visitor Services
640-Mullis Street, Suite 210-211
Friday Harbor, Washington 98250
(888) 468-3701

JEKYLL ISLAND

Visitor Services
100 – James Road
Jekyll Island, Georgia 31527
(912) 635-2236

FANTASTIC CRUISES
To Consider

CRYSTAL CRUISE LINE
(888) 722-002
"Luxury cruising with innovative excellence"

DISNEY CRUISE LINE
(800) 951-3532
"The enchantment is seemingly endless."

SEABOURN CRUISE LINE
(866) 755-5619
"Ultra luxury cruising"

CHARMING CARRIAGE RIDES

To Consider

KC'S CLASSIC CARRIAGE CO., LLC

Scottsdale, Arizona

(602) 540-1234

"Providing memories that last a life time"

76 CARRIAGE CO.

Philadelphia, Pennsylvania

(215) 923-8516

"Providing Philadelphia with superior tours"

SAVANNAH CARRIAGE TOUR COMPANY

Savannah, Georgia

(912) 443-9333

"Will take you through this beautiful city"

OUTSTANDING MUSEUMS

To Consider

J. PAUL GETTY MUSEUM

1200 – Getty Center Drive
Los Angeles, CA 90048-1687
(310) 440-7330

ART INSTITUTE OF CHICAGO

111 S. Michigan Avenue
Chicago, Ill 60603
(312) 443-3600

SMITHSONIAN AMERICAN ART MUSEUM

8 TH and F Street, N.W.
Washington, D.C. 20004
(202) 633-1000

CAPTIVATING
THEATRES
To Consider

THE SMITH CENTER
361- Symphony Park Avenue
Las Vegas, Nevada 89106
(702) 749-2000

MCCARTER THEATRE CENTER
91-University Place
Princeton, New Jersey 08540
(609) 258-2787

GOODSPEED OPERA HOUSE
6 Main Street
East Haddam, Connecticut 06423
(860) 873-8668

TERRIFIC FUN PLACES TO VISIT

To Consider

THE HENRY FORD
Fun Village, Museum, Tour
20900 - Oakwood Boulevard
Dearborn, Michigan 48124-5029
(313) 982-6001

WALT DISNEY WORLD
Fun Magic Kingdom
Visitor Center
3111-World Drive
Orlando, Florida 32830
(407) 939-5277

WARNER BROTHERS STUDIO
Fun Tour, Perfect Towns, Old West
Tour Center
3400-West Riverside Drive
Burbank, California 91505
(877) 492-8687

ABOUT THE AUTHOR

Lynne Thomas, M.A. is an expert in the field of marriage and
relationships. She shares a valuable
collection of talents in her career in
psychology. Lynne began her career
as an inspired psychotherapist and
marriage counselor. For thirty years,
she assisted a host of married couples
to enrich, elevate, and improve their
marriages.

A captivating speaker, a proficient
seminar leader, and insightful author,
Lynne has dedicated her life to
helping married couples. She created a successful practical
method to help couples create an amazing marriage and
enduring love.

As an author, Lynne has written two very thought-
provoking books. In addition, eager to share her knowledge, she
wrote an insightful monthly newspaper column for over ten
years as well as a monthly newsletter. After experiencing a
miracle, Lynne's profound gratitude prompted her to author
two Bible studies.

Now, *A Love Forever: Creating An Amazing Marriage is*
Lynne's gift to you and your marriage. It is her hope that you
will use this resource to assist you in creating an amazing
marriage and love forever.

Visit www.marriageamazing.com
For other valuable resources, videos, trainings and
more.

*Joy does not exactly happen to us. We have
to make a choice and select joy,
and keep selecting it each day.*
~ Henri Nouwen

A Love Forever
Creating An *Amazing* Marriage

Please spread the word about **A Love Forever**.

My passion is to transform marriages,
inspire enduring love, and
encourage fantastic experiences.

Thank You!

For information about purchasing additional books,
seminars, and speaking arrangements contact:

lakeshore.press@ymail.com

or

www.marriageamazing.com